YOUR KNOWLEDGE HAS VALUE

Bibliographic information published by the German National Library:

The German National Library lists this publication in the National Bibliography; detailed bibliographic data are available on the Internet at http://dnb.dnb.de .

Imprint:

Copyright © 2016 GRIN Verlag, Open Publishing GmbH
Print and binding: Books on Demand GmbH, Norderstedt Germany
ISBN: 9783668371682

This book at GRIN:

http://www.grin.com/en/e-book/349852/convolutional-neural-network-in-classifying-scanned-documents

Tai Doan

Convolutional Neural Network in classifying scanned documents

GRIN Publishing

GRIN - Your knowledge has value

Since its foundation in 1998, GRIN has specialized in publishing academic texts by students, college teachers and other academics as e-book and printed book. The website www.grin.com is an ideal platform for presenting term papers, final papers, scientific essays, dissertations and specialist books.

Visit us on the internet:

http://www.grin.com/

http://www.facebook.com/grincom

http://www.twitter.com/grin_com

University of Science and Technology of Hanoi

Information and Communication Technology Department

M1 Internship Report

Academic year 2015 - 2016

Document classification using Convolutional Neural Networks

---

presented by

Tai Tien DOAN

registered at Université de Rennes 1

Host organization : ICTLab USTH

Hanoi - Vietnam

Acknowledgements

This internship project consumed a huge amount of work, research and dedication. Still, the implementation would not have been possible if I had not had the support of many individuals and organizations. Therefore, I would like to extend my sincere gratitude to all of them.

The project was supported by the University of Science and Technology of Hanoi, especially the ICTLab of the university. I am thankful to my supervisor, Dr. Tung Hoang TRAN, who has kindly guided and supported me even before the project began.

I am thankful to Dr. Mai Chi LUONG, who spent time talking with me and gave me helpful advices on my academic orientation.

I am also grateful to all professors and researchers in ICTLab for providing me such a good working environment, devices and discussions.

I also would like to say thanks to Marie Ballere and Romain Verset, two students from France, who spent time discussing with me and helped me to understand better my problems.

I have to express my appreciation to all members in my family. They are my source of encouragement and wisdom.

Nevertheless, I would like to give praises and thanks to God for leading me to the university and giving me strength to overcome all difficulties in my study and life.

Asbtract

In this project, I created and augmented a dataset from a number of given images to train and test convolutional neural network which is used to classify five classes of images of scanned documents. In order to generate the dataset, some image processing techniques were applied such as sliding-window, rotating, flipping and pyramid-sizing. The result of this phase is a set of images having same size 244x224x3. These images after being labeled were divided into three dataset for training, validating and testing the network. The network is a simple convolution neural network which is also called LeNet. It has three convolutional layers and one fully connected layer. After being trained and validated, the best state of the network was pointed out and tested on the testing dataset and some real images. The result showed that the LeNet was able to classify images of documents in a pretty high accuracy. At the end of the project, I modified the network and discussed the affect that those changes had on the network with the purpose of creating another similar network which can perform better than the original one. The result proved that it worked a little better than its original version.

Contents

1 **Introduction**   2
  1.1 Context   2
    1.1.1 About ICTLab   2
    1.1.2 ARCHIVES project   2
    1.1.3 Internship context   2
  1.2 Report organization   3

2 **State of the art**   4
  2.1 Artificial intelligence & machine learning   4
  2.2 Artificial neural network (ANN)   4
    2.2.1 History   4
    2.2.2 Regular neural network   5
    2.2.3 Convolutional neural network (LeNet)   7
    2.2.4 Training and evaluating 10

3 **Contribution**   12
  3.1 Data creation and augmentation 12
    3.1.1 ARCHIVES dataset 12
    3.1.2 Creating data 12
    3.1.3 Augmenting the data 15
    3.1.4 Summary and Result 16
  3.2 Constructing the convolution neural network (LeNet) 17
    3.2.1 The model 17
    3.2.2 Preparing data 17
    3.2.3 Training 18
    3.2.4 Validation and testing 19
  3.3 Developing the network 20

4 **Results**   21
  4.1 The basic network 21
    4.1.1 Testing on the dataset 21
    4.1.2 Testing on real images 22
  4.2 The network modifications 23
    4.2.1 Fully connected layer 23
    4.2.2 Convolutional layers 23
  4.3 The new network 23

5 **Conclusion**   25

A **Transfer functions**   26

List of Figures

2.1 A single-input neuron (left) and a multiple-input neuron (right) [5]   5
2.2 Three-layer neural network [5]   6
2.3 Logistic sigmoid (blue), hyperbolic tangent with recommend parameters (green) and ReLU
     (red)   7
2.4 Typical CNN architecture [2]   8
2.5 Convolution [10]   9
2.6 Dropout Neural Net Model [18] 10
2.7 Underfitting (left), good fit (middle) and overfitting (right) [3] 11

3.1 Sliding window 13
3.2 Sub-images generated by sliding window 14
3.3 A blank window (188.jpg on the left) 14
3.4 Choosing bounding box in matlab 15
3.5 An original image and its 5 degrees rotations 16
3.6 Combination of flipping and orthogonal rotating 16
3.7 Training accuracy and validation accuracy 19

4.1 Training accuracy and Validation accuracy 21
4.2 Test images and their output given by the network 22
4.3 Network accuracy under the effect of fully connected layer's width 23
4.4 Network accuracy under the effect of convolution kernels 24
4.5 Training accuracy comparison between the original network and the new network 24

List of Tables

I   Number of images used in each class 13

II   Number of generated sub-images in each class 17

III   Table of layers in the LeNet and their size. 17

IV   Number of sub-images in 5 classes participating the dataset 17

V   Number of sub-images in 5 classes participating in one data file 18

VI   Testing accuracy of the network on classes (%) 22

VII   Test images and their output given by the network 23

VIII Transfer functions [5] 26

1

Chapter 1

Introduction

This chapter contains the information about the context of the project, the lab that I was working during my internship and the motivation of this project. After that, the structure of this report is also explained.

1.1 Context

This section introduces the ICTLab where I have been doing my internship, the ARCHIVES project that I had chance to participated and the context of my internship.

1.1.1 About ICTLab

During three months of my M1 internship, I had an opportunity to work in the ICTLab[8] of University of Science and Technology of Hanoi (USTH), an international laboratory joint between USTH and partners coming from Vietnam and French such as Institute of Information Technology (IOIT) Hanoi, Institut de Recherche pour le Développement (IRD) and the University of La Rochelle, France.

ICTLab was found in 2014 under the support of USTH, French Embassy in Vietnam, Asian Development Bank (ADB) and some universities and institutes from France.

Currently, the lab is working on two main projects:

- **SWARMS**: Say and Watch: Automated image/sound Recognition for Mobile monitoring Systems.

- **ARCHIVES**: Analysis and Reconstruction of Catastrophes in History within Interactive Virtual Environments and Simulations. This project is also the one that I participated.

1.1.2 ARCHIVES project

The aim of ARCHIVES is to extract data and information from collected historical documents to provide a virtual representation which would help researches to understand more about natural disasters in the past on the area of Red River. By researching on such great presentation, researchers can improve the prediction and management of the natural hazards which may happen in the future.

1.1.3 Internship context

One of the initial steps in project ARCHIVES is extracting data from documents. However, these documents are not in the same type. They are divided into five classes: graph, map, photo, hand-written text and printed text. To effectively extract data from these documents, each type of document must be treated by using a suitable method. Thus, the very first step of the project is classifying all documents that have been collected and new ones in the future.

At the moment, among different methods which have been applied for classifying images, convolution neural network (CNN) is one of the best. In this project, I learned CNN and applied this method to create a classifier for ARCHIVES data.

In detail, my work in this internship project was divided into two parts:

- Data augmentation and creation for training learning a classification model
- Training a classifying model using convolutional neural network

All works I have done in these two parts are explained in detail in Chapter 3: Contribution.

1.2 Report organization

This report is divided into five main chapters. The first chapter contains some introduction information related to my internship. In the next chapter: "State of the art", I explained some concepts which should be understood before starting working with convolutional neural network. Chapter three: "Contribution" describes all works that I have done in project and after that, the results are shown and discussed in the forth chapter: "Results". Finally, everything is summed up in the last chapter: "Conclusion".

Chapter 2

State of the art

In this chapter, before explaining the convolutional neural network, some basic concepts of artificial intelligence and machine learning has been introduced, then the artificial neural network - the supper-set of convolution neural network - with its algorithm and components has been described. After that, I explained the convolutional neural network and discussed its advantages over regular neural networks on learning images.

At the end of this chapter, I also explained two important problems called underfitting and overfitting, which appear when training learning models like the ones in this project.

2.1 Artificial intelligence & machine learning

Machine learning is a sub-set of artificial intelligence (AI). However, due to the growth and extension of machine learning, the boundary between machine learning and artificial intelligence is becoming very blurred.

The goal of AI is to mimic some special functions of humans brain [16] such as speech recognition and problem solving. Many methods have been created to solve these problems and machine learning is one of these. Just like the name, machine learning focuses on making the computer "learn" from experiences.

In 1997, Tom Mitchell introduced a formal definition of machine learning: *"A computer program is said to learn from experience E with respect to some class of tasks T and performance measure P if its performance at tasks in T, as measured by P, improves with experience E."*[13]

Before starting to learn, a model has no pre-knowledge of the problem, but it is allowed to try to solve a problem with a set of initial variables. Those values can be set or picked randomly and have no relation to the expected output of the model. As a sequence, the model will fail many times to give the right answer, but after each time, the model modifies itself to get a better answer for the problem. Finally, the machine will be able to solve not only the problem it was given but also similar problems, depending on the regularity of the model.

2.2 Artificial neural network (ANN)

Inspired by the biological neural networks of human and animal brain, the artificial neural network inherits some advantages of this structure so that it is able to implement some tasks that the brain does. At the moment, the ANN cannot work perfectly as humans brain in all fields, but the number of valuable applications of ANN has been increasing a lot, not only in computer science but in many other areas such as economics, finance, environment and so on.

2.2.1 History

Learning is a function of humans brain which is made of a system of neurons. Inspired by this biological system, in 1943, McCulloch and Pitts [12] created a computational model named Threshold Logic Unit

(TLU) which is believed as the beginning of artificial neural network.

A few years later, Donald Hebb introduced his theory called Hebb's rule [6] which explained how the repetition of a connection between two cells in a neural network affects the wire's strength. In a short way, Siegrid Löwel's said: "Neurons wire together if they fire together"[11]. This is considered as the 'typical' unsupervised learning rule.

In 1958, Frank Rosenblatt [15] explained the perceptron algorithm for supervised learning of binary classifier. The algorithm implemented simple mathematical operations on a computer learning network with two layers. Because of the limitation of the perceptron algorithm, the circuits as exclusive-or (XOR) could not be processed by neural networks until 1974, when Paul Werbos [20] invented the back-propagation algorithm. The back-propagation algorithm solved the XOR problem which leads to the age of quick training multilayer neural networks.

Due to the development of computing technology, it can be assured that the performance of ANN will continue raising and will be applied in most of areas in our lives.

2.2.2 Regular neural network

There are some types of neural network. In this subsection, the most traditional type called the fully connected neural network will be explained.

2.2.2.1 Neuron model

Neuron is the most basic unit in the neural network and single-input neuron is the most simple form of neuron.

Figure 2.1, on the left, is the image of a single-input neuron.

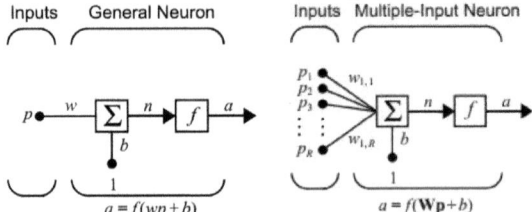

Figure 2.1: A single-input neuron (left) and a multiple-input neuron (right) [5]

Two scalar p and w respectively are the input and weight of the neuron. After being multiplied with each other, the result is summed with the other input which had been created by multiplying number 1 with a bias b. The output n of the summer is sent to the transfer function f providing a which is the scalar output of the neuron. In short, the neuron output is computed as:

$$a = f(wp + b)$$

In reality, most of the neurons in artificial neural networks receive not only one input but multiple inputs as showed on the right side of Figure 2.1.

A multiple-input neuron receives more than one input and each of these inputs is multiplied by a weight. After that, the result is sent to the summer to be added with bias b and just like in single-input neuron, the output n of the summer is brought to the transfer function and finally, the neuron gives an output a which is also a scalar.

A layer of neural network is constructed from one or multiple neurons and a network is constructed from one or more layers. The Figure 2.2 in the next page exposes the structure of a three-layer artificial neural network.

5

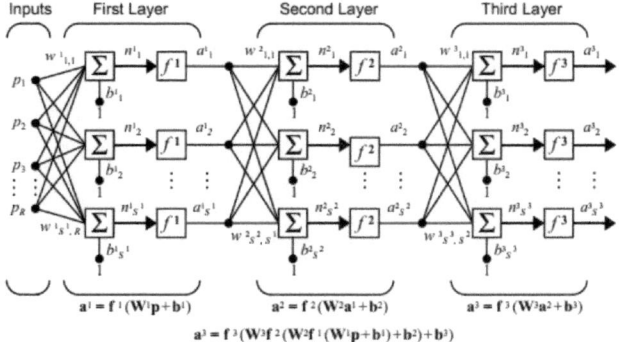

Figure 2.2: Three-layer neural network [5]

2.2.2.2 Transfer functions

Transfer functions, or activation functions, which were found in figures of neurons we have seen previously, are very important components of the learning network. They transform the result of each neuron to a more valuable form, especially transforming from linear to non-linear numbers. (Appendix A)

Some most popular activation functions are:

- **Logistic sigmoid:**

$$f(x) = \frac{1}{1 + e^{-x}}$$

The logistic sigmoid function used to be known as the most popular activation function for artificial neural networks to introduce non-linearity in the model due to its biologically plausibility, regardless hyperbolic tangent function performed better in practical problems.

- **Hyperbolic tangent**

$$f(x) = tanh(x)$$

The hyperbolic tangent function performs better than the traditional logistic sigmoid when training multilayer neural networks in practical works, especially with suitable parameters[9]:

$$f(x) = 1.7159 * tanh(\frac{2}{3}x)$$

However, hyperbolic tangent function does not model the biological nodes as well as logistic sigmoid, it could not take the first position of logistic sigmoid.

- **Rectified Linear Units (ReLU)**

The story changed when Rectified Linear Units was introduced by Nair and Hinton [14] in 2010 and just one year later, it was claimed as a better model model of the biological neurons and performed better than the previous methods[4].

The ReLU operation, in fact, is very simple:

$$f(x) = \max(0, x)$$

Figure 2.3 compares graphic expression of the three transfer functions below:

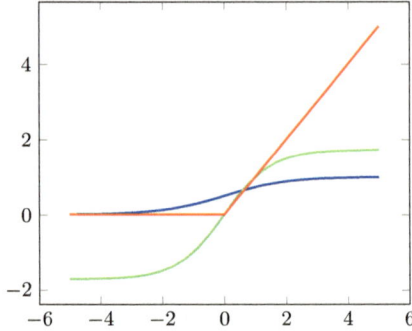

Figure 2.3: Logistic sigmoid (blue), hyperbolic tangent with recommend parameters (green) and ReLU (red)

2.2.2.3 Backpropagation

In terms of pattern recognition[17], it is known that analyzing features of input images is a very important task. At the time when pattern recognition method was born, these features were designed by human engineers. However, human-engineered features are very limit and generating features by hand in fact is an exhausted work, so computer scientists have been trying to create multilayer networks that can proactively learn features from data. And the key of training multilayer networks is backpropagation.

Backpropagation, or backward propagation of errors is usually used with gradient descent or another optimization method to train ANNs. The method computes gradient of a loss function regarding to all weights of the multilayer network. This is actually an application of the derivatives' chain rule. The idea is that, we can compute derivative of the objective regarding to the input of a module by computing derivation of the output of that module and then moving backwards[9] through the module. Applying the same operation for the whole network, starting from the output and all the way to the input, the gradients can be computed regarding to the weights of each module.

Based on these gradients, the optimization function will update the weights in order to minimize result of the loss function. Repeating the process many times, the model would have a set of weights which provides an output similar to the expected result.

2.2.3 Convolutional neural network (LeNet)

Convolutional neural network (CNN, also called ConvNet) is a subset of artificial neural network. While classical neural networks are inspired by the system of nodes (neurons) in animal brain, convolutional neural networks are inspired by the structure of the animal visual cortex[7], in which, neurons are organized as overlapping sub-regions titling the visual field. Those sub-regions are called receptive fields[1].

The receptive fields have various sizes. Cells which contain large receptive fields work as local filters over the input space while other cells contain smaller receptive fields tend to recognize edge-like patterns observed by the fields[7]. This property makes the ConvNet be able to automatically detect features from inputs, rather than depending on features engineered by human. This is a great advantage of CNN over classical ANNs which contain only fully connected layers.

Figure 2.4 displays the typical architecture of a CNN.

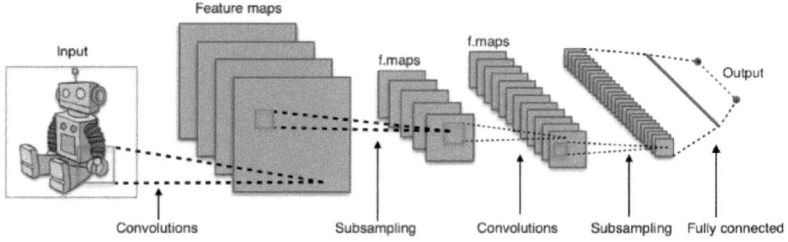

Figure 2.4: Typical CNN architecture [2]

2.2.3.1 Properties

Previously, it is known that classical multilayer perception (MLP) of ANN models have the structure of fully connected nodes. This organization worked very well with low-dimensional data but had a serious problem with high-dimensional data, which known as the "Curse of dimensionality"[19].

CNNs, in the other hand, which was designed to emulate the behaviour of a visual cortex, can overcome the problem of MLP networks because of the ability to detect the spatially local correlation appear in images.

There are three main differences of CNN with regular ANN:

- **3D volumes of neurons:** Neurons in layers of CNN are organized in a 3D structure: width, height and depth.

- **Local connectivity:** In CNN, neurons of nearby layers are connected as local patterns and this property makes the network be able to exploit the spatially local correlation from the images.

- **Shared weights:** Every filter in CNN is replicated on the entire visual field where they share the same weight vector and bias. Therefore, the same feature can be detected from anywhere on a convolutional layer.

2.2.3.2 Main layers

A Convolution neural network is constructed of two parts: features extraction and classification.

- **Features extraction:** The features extraction part of CNNs usually contain three main layers:

    - **Convolutional layer:** Before starting to explain the convolutional layer in CNN, the convolution operation must be clearly understood. After that, I will explain the convolutional layer.
        * **Convolution:** Convolution is a technique used widely in image processing area. The method is the foundation of many image filters such as blur, sharpen and edge-detection. Each convolution has a kernel. Width and height of kernels must always be odd numbers and they usually have the same value. Convolutions is a per-pixel operation applied on a source image. Figure 2.5 explains how the convolution kernel operates on a pixel. Normally, the kernel starts from the top-left corner of the source image, then moves to the right side and downward until it covers the whole image. Each step, the kernel hovers an area equal to its size on the source image, multiplies its values element-wise with the area on the source image, then sums them up and results a value on the destination pixel. All the computed destination pixels together form a new image which is the result of the convolution. The position of the destination pixel is corresponding to the center of the

8

kernel, so the size of the result image will be smaller than the source image. However, those pixel can be easily recovered because the important information of image usually lays on the center area, not some pixels on the edge.

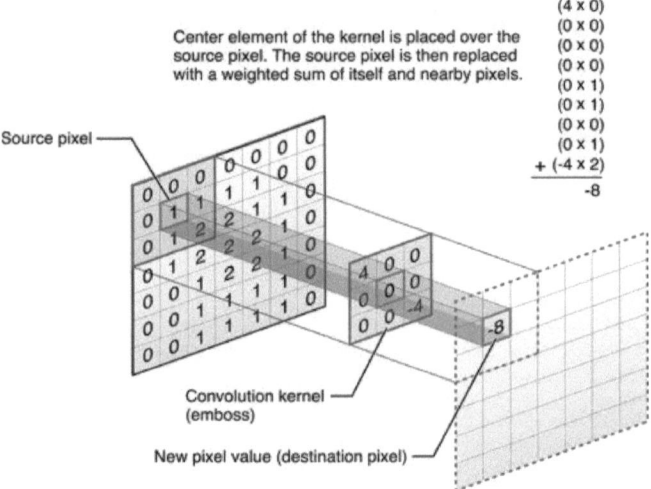

Figure 2.5: Convolution [10]

* **Convolutional layer in CNN:** Convolutional layers are the key components in CNNs. Convolutional layers perform convolution operation across the input volume and consist a cube of neurons. The depth of this cube depends on the number of channels in the input volume.

  This neurons are the result of the convolution operation of the kernels of the layer on the input volume. Each neuron is connected to a specific zone on of the input called receptive field. For example, on the first convolution layer of the network, RGB images which have size 224x224x3, are the inputs. The kernel size is 3x3, so the receptive field it hovers on the input is 3x3, too. As a result, each neuron in the convolution layer is connected to a region of 3x3x3 on the input, hence it has 27 weighted inputs which are trained and updated after each training iteration.

- **ReLU layer:** The reLU layer, as described in the previous section acts as an activation for the output of the CNN neurons.

- **Pooling layer:** The pooling layer is usually put in between convolutional layers in CNN, to reduce the size of the input volume for the next convolutional layer. The pooling layer only affect height and width dimension of the volume, not the the depth.

  The most common pooling method used in CNN is max-pooling. The operation is performed in each depth slice of the input volume. For example, the input volume which is 224x224x3 is applied max-pooling with window-size is 2x2. The input will be considered as 3 slices of 224x224. Each slide will be divided into non-overlapping regions 2x2, and the highest value in each region will be the max-pool value. The output of this max-pool has size 112x112x3.

  The property of pooling layer is very useful in avoiding overfitting problem, because it reduce the number of weight in the network. It is also reduce the computational complexity for the following layers in the network.

– **Dropout layer:** Dropout is another effective method used for avoiding overfitting in CNNs. The technique can be applied for both fully connected layers and convolutional layers.

The phrase "dropout"[18] refers to dropping out neurons from a neural network. Dropping a neuron out means temporarily removing it, along with all its incoming and outgoing connections from the network. Figure 2.6 is an example of applying dropout on a fully connected neural network with two hidden layers.

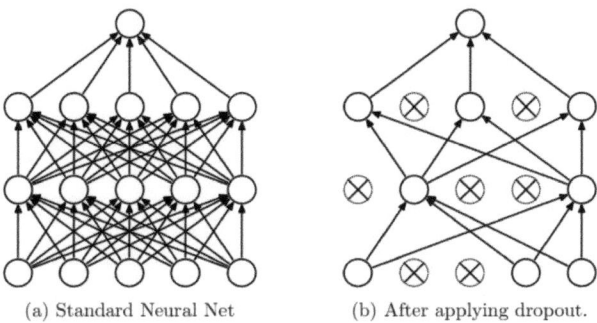

(a) Standard Neural Net   (b) After applying dropout.

Figure 2.6: Dropout Neural Net Model [18]

- **Classification:** In LeNet, the classification part normally contain only one or two fully connected layers.
    - **Fully connected layer:** The fully connected layers in CNNs work exactly the same as ones in other ANNs. They are usually located at the end of the network to compute the class scores.

    Some larger CNNs which contains tens or hundreds of convolutional layers, more fully connected layers can be added and going along with them there can be ReLU or pooling layers.

2.2.4 Training and evaluating

The process of training and evaluating a learning network has the following steps:

2.2.4.1 Preparing dataset

For training a learning network, especially CNN, a lot of data is required. However, not all of these data get involved in the training process. The dataset must be separated to 3 parts:

- **Training dataset:** The network learns only from this dataset and tries to fit to this dataset.

- **Validation dataset:** After a certain of time, the network accuracy is checked using this dataset.

- **Testing dataset:** Based on the validation accuracy, the best model is chosen and tested with this dataset. The testing accuracy is considered as the official performance of the network.

2.2.4.2 Training the network

As it is impossible to feed the network with all samples in the training dataset at once, we have to train it with small set of samples called batches.

The training dataset can be used to trained the network more than one time. Theoretically, the training accuracy (the network's accuracy computed using the training dataset) will increase because the network becomes fitter to the training data. However, having a network which is too fit to the training data is not always good. The reason is described below.

2.2.4.3 Underfitting & overfitting

Underfitting and overfitting are two concepts using to describe networks performance.

- **Underfitting** takes place when a network performs poorly on any dataset. Networks are usually underfitting when they just start learning the training dataset.

- **Overfitting** occurs when a networks is too fit to the training dataset while has low performance in testing data.

A good network should not be underfitting or overfitting, but in somewhere in between. The Figure 2.7 visualizes how a "good fit" network performs on a 2d data, comparing to underfitting and overfitting.

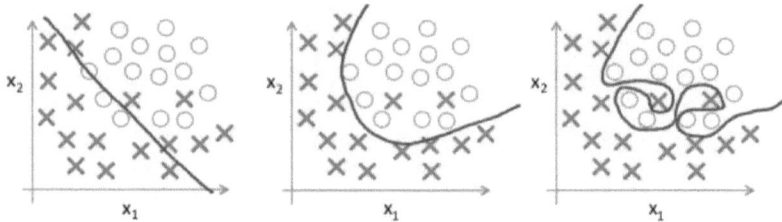

Figure 2.7: Underfitting (left), good fit (middle) and overfitting (right) [3]

11

Chapter 3

Contribution

In order to build a CNN classifier, it need to be trained with labeled data until it was able to classify images of for the ARCHIVES project. Thus, the first step was creating a set of data which was labeled by human, then creating a CNN model and using the dataset to train, validate and test the model until the testing result is acceptable. At that point, the model would "understand" the different features between samples of 5 classes and be able to classify new documents which are not in the training dataset. Below are the details of what I have done in those tasks.

3.1 Data creation and augmentation

Training a model requires a lot of training data. Not only about quantity, the quality of learning data is also very important. If the input data is not good, the training process will not succeed. In this section, I explained all steps I have done to create and augment data for the training model in the next section.

3.1.1 ARCHIVES dataset

The dataset of ARCHIVES project was a large set of images created by scanning documents which contain the data related to the Red River in the history. There are totally 3789 files which are all images. Most of them are colored images.

Based on the aim of ARCHIVES project, those images would be divided into 5 classes: graph, map, photo, hand-written text and printed text, but they were all mixed together when I received.

In terms of size, A4 documents take the largest percentage of the dataset and resized to 1024 in width. Some maps, photos, graph and telegraphs have different sizes but they are just a small part compared to A4 papers.

3.1.2 Creating data

The LeNet in the next step requires fixed size input data, so it is not possible to just put the raw images to the model. The objective of this step is to create usable data from the given raw images.

3.1.2.1 Labeling

The method used to create this learning model was supervised learning, so all input images must be divided into 5 expected classes by human before being used for training the model. At the beginning, all input images were put in the same directory. I created 5 directories respectively named to 5 classes, then moved images to the suitable class directory.

Although the task was simple and easy but the dataset was very large (3789 images), it took a lot of time to classify (and then process) the whole data. Moreover, in the next steps, each image would be processed to generate other transformations (flipping, rotation and so on) then cut down into smaller sub-images, so the amount of data would increase a lot. Therefore, just a part of the image set would be enough to feed my learning model.

Table I displays the number of images used in each class.

Graph	Map	Photo	Hand-written text	Printed text	Total
30	25	52	50	50	207

Table I: Number of images used in each class

3.1.2.2 Sliding window

In reality, when looking at an image of a scanned document, we do not have to look into every detail to say which kind of document it is, but usually only one area of the image is enough. It means that if we cut that image into pieces, and if those pieces are big enough, then most of them will contain enough information to be well-classified.

Furthermore, the CNN in the next section requires all input to have the same size, so the solution applied in this case is a sliding window. The size of the window would be the size of the input data for the CNN model. In this project, I chose 224x224x3 (x3 because of 3 channels of RGB images).

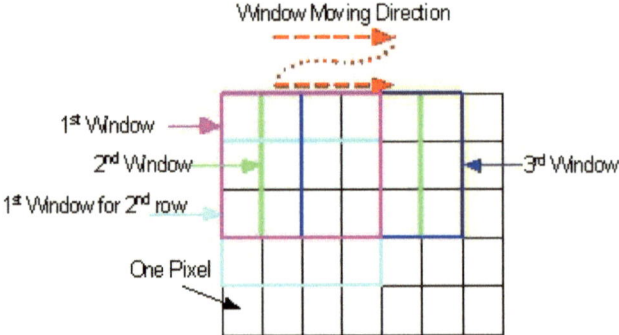

Figure 3.1: Sliding window

Figure 3.1 shows how the sliding window worked. It started at the top left of the image. Each step, it moved to the right a specified distance (112 pixels in this case). When the window reached the right edge of the image, it came back to the left, not the previous position but shifted down 112 pixels. The loop was repeated until the window slide touch the bottom right corner of the image, then it started with another image.

Anywhere the window stopped, it took all the pixels it was covering to create a new sub-image file. Those created sub-images would be used as inputs of the CNN model. In the Figure 3.2 a group of sub-images generated by sliding window approach are displayed.

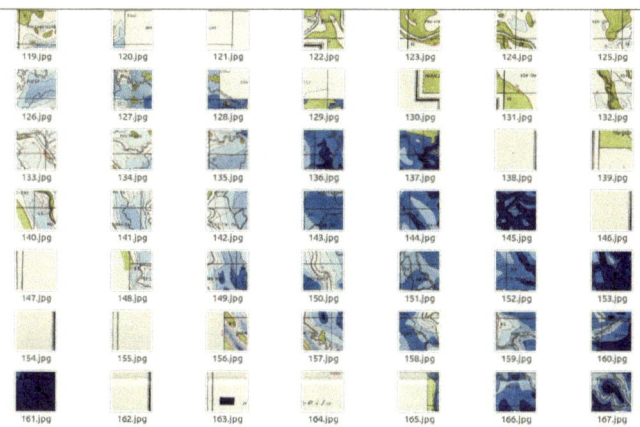

Figure 3.2: Sub-images generated by sliding window

3.1.2.3 Bounding boxes

After applying sliding window approach, I realized that there was a trouble: many sub-images are impossible to be classified because they are the image's parts which contain no structural information such as blank areas (188.jpg in Figure 3.3). Consequently, it need to define one or some scopes for the sliding window on each image.

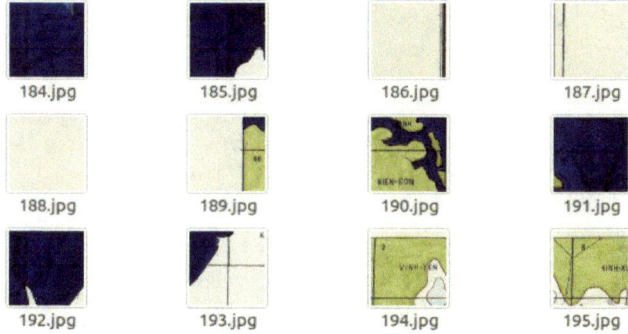

Figure 3.3: A blank window (188.jpg on the left)

In order to do that, I created an interface displaying images one by one and manually defined the bounding-boxes on the images by clicking on each image (Figure 3.4). A bounding-box is defined by 2 clicks: the first one defines top-left corner of the bounding-box and the second one defines its bottom-right corner.

The coordinates of bounding-boxes' corners are stored in a text files. After that, another program read those coordinates, applied sliding window in the bounding boxes of each images and generated 224x224x3 sub-images.

If a bounding-box had been smaller than sliding window in any side, it would have been ignored.

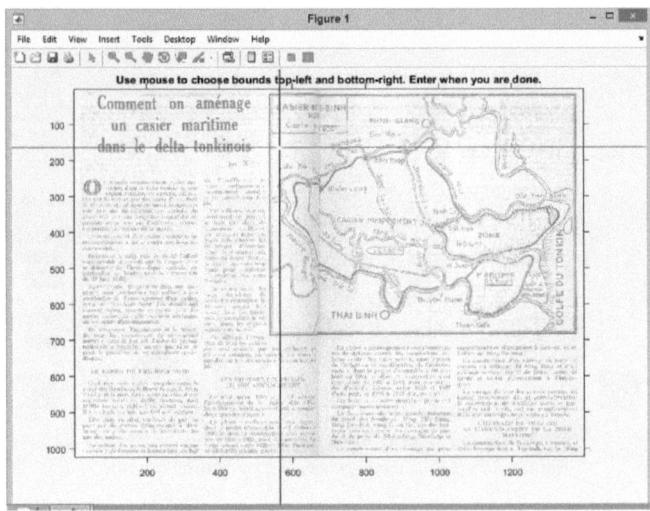

Figure 3.4: Choosing bounding box in matlab

3.1.3 Augmenting the data

We know that the more various the training data is, the more accurate it can classify in the future, but rather than adding more images into the dataset, I firstly tried to extract as much information from the dataset as possible. This can be done by applying some simple transformations on the images.

3.1.3.1 Pyramid re-sizing

The first way to increase diversity of the dataset is to resize its images. If all printed-text documents in the dataset have the same font-size, it will be very difficult for the model to recognize texts which have different sizes. This is true for images of documents in all 5 classes.

In the dataset, all of the images have at least one side greater than 1024, so I re-sized them to 3 other sizes 1024 pixels, 512 pixels and 256 pixels. At this point, the dataset was 4 times increased. However, it is not always exactly 4 times because the size of sliding window is 224x224x3, so if the size of the chosen bounding box was smaller than the sliding window, then that image would be ignored. This can happen to image which has size of 512 pixels or 256 pixels.

3.1.3.2 Rotating

The second way to increase dataset size is rotating. It is actually a common problem when we scan documents. It happens when a sheet is not put straight in the scanner. Sometimes, the rotation is only a few degrees, but sometimes it can be 90 degree or 180 degree depending on how we put it in the scanner. Another reason to add rotating forms of images to the dataset is that even when we rotate a document (map, photo, graph, hand-written text or written text) we still can tell which type of document it is, because the unique structure of the curves and lines of that class is still recognizable.

In total, I applied rotation -5 and +5 degrees (non-orthogonal) on all original images (Figure 3.5), then rotated them by +90, -90 and +180 degrees (orthogonally). The non-orthogonal rotation increased the number of images 3 folds and the orthogonal rotation made it up 4 folds.

Figure 3.5: An original image and its 5 degrees rotations

The order of implementing these operation is also a very important thing. Orthogonal rotations can be easily applied on each sub-images after sliding window, but the non-orthogonal rotations cannot be applied that way. I also cannot apply them after choosing bounding boxes because it is impossible to store coordinates of an 5-degrees-rotated rectangle with only points. Thus, I applied +-5 degree rotations before the step of bounding boxes. Then, they would be displayed to let a person click on them to define bounding boxes as an original image.

3.1.3.3 Flipping

The purpose of adding flipped images to the dataset is similar to rotation. When an image is flipping, the content is changed but the properties of structures of curves and lines on the image remains the same, and the model classifies images according to their structures, not the contents. Just like orthogonal rotating, the method flipping can be implemented right on sub-images after sliding window.

Flipping up-down and left-right increase the number of images by 4 times. However, applying orthogonal rotating and flipping separately will cause redundancy, so they were combined. Figure 3.6 is an example of applying flipping and orthogonal rotation together.

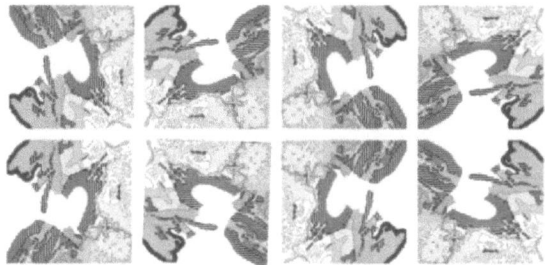

Figure 3.6: Combination of flipping and orthogonal rotating

Applying rotating and flipping on the whole dataset, each image has 7 more forms. This means the size of the dataset is increased 8-folds.

3.1.4 Summary and Result

In summary, the whole process of Data augmentation can be described as below:

- **Labeling**: dividing images into 5 classes directories

- **Pyramid re-sizing**: adding 3 more resized versions of every images (1024, 512 and 256 pixels at the long side)

- **Non-orthogonal rotating**: adding 2 more (+-5 degrees) rotated versions of every image

- **Bounding boxes**: user clicking on each image to define bounding boxes

- **Sliding window**: sliding on bounding boxes areas on each image, generating sub-images

- **Flipping and orthogonal rotating**: adding 7 more versions of each sub-image by combining flipping and orthogonal rotating

After applying all of those steps resulted set of sub-images put in 5 classes. The Table II displays the amount of sub-images in each of those classes.

Graph	Map	Photo	Hand-written text	Printed text	Total
4000	3904	8560	7560	38376	62400

Table II: Number of generated sub-images in each class

3.2 Constructing the convolution neural network (LeNet)

3.2.1 The model

The convolution neural network is constructed from 3 convolution layers sized respectively 3x3, 3x3 and 5x5, 2 pooling layers both in size 2x2, 1 fully-connected layer width 200704 and one read-out layer width 32. The network is described in the following table.

Layer	Operation	Layer size	Output size
Input data	load data		100,224,224,3
Conv1	Data*W1 + b1	3,3,16	100,224,224,16
ReLU			
Conv2	Conv1*W2 + b2	3,3,32	100,224,224,32
ReLU			
MP1	maxpool_2x2(Conv2)	2,2	100,112,112,32
Conv3	MP1*W3 + b3	5,5,64	100,112,112,64
ReLU			
MP2	maxpool_2x2(Conv3)	2,2	100,56,56,64
MP2R	flattening		100,56*56*64
FC	MP2R x W4 + b4	32	100,32
Read-out	FC x W5 + b5	5	100,5

Table III: Table of layers in the LeNet and their size.

3.2.2 Preparing data

On Table II, the number of sub-images in class printed-text was much higher than the other, and such difference would be not good for training the network. Thus, I took randomly only 15000 samples from the printed-text to involve the training data. The number of sub-images from 5 classes involving the dataset were listed in the following table.

Graph	Map	Photo	Hand-written text	Printed text	Total
4000	3904	8560	7560	15000	39204

Table IV: Number of sub-images in 5 classes participating the dataset

I could start training the network at this moment, however, there was a problem about performance here. In order to feed the network, the computer would have to load thousands of image files, one by one, and it would take a lot of time. Hence, the solution was to combine images into larger data files, so it would take less time when the dataset is loaded. Those data files should not be too large either, to not cause out-of-memory error. Finally, I chose to group samples in files which include 1300 samples (200MB) in each. From 39204 samples (Table IV), 30 files were created. Those files would be used for training, validating and testing the LeNet model.

Another point about those data files is that, percentage of sample from any class in each data file should be the same percentage in the whole dataset. For instance, in 39204 samples of the whole dataset, class graph has 4000 samples, took 10.2 percents, so in 1300 samples of one data files the class graph must also take 10.2 percents, which means 133 files. This property helped stabilizing the training process.

The number of samples of 5 class in one data file is listed in Table V.

Graph	Map	Photo	Hand-written text	Printed text	Total
133	133	285	252	500	1300

Table V: Number of sub-images in 5 classes participating in one data file

Each data file contains a tensor having size (1300,244,244,3). Along with creating data files, I also created label files which contain labels of samples in the data files. Each label file contains a vector 1300 long, storing values varying from 0 to 4, presenting 5 classes.

When 30 data files were ready, I divided them into 3 groups, and of course, the respective label files went with them.

- Training: 15 files (50% of dataset)

- validation: 10 files (33% of dataset)

- Testing: 5 files (17% of dataset)

3.2.3 Training

After declaring the model graph and initializing variables, the process of training the model started and as was mentioned above, the model was trained with each file. As the model could not receive 1300 samples at a time, so after loading and normalizing all samples in the file, it had to mix-up all those samples, divided them into 13 batches of 100 samples, then learned those batches one by one.

The normalization algorithm was simple and described as the following pseudo code:

$$dataset\_sub = dataset - mean(dataset)$$

$$dataset = \frac{dataset\_sub}{standart\_deviation(dataset\_sub)}$$

The "learn" step is the key of the training process, however it was not very complex because TensorFlow had provided useful functions for it. Each time the session.run() function was fired, a set of instructions were implemented. Firstly, the batch of sample was sent to the model's input to compute prediction outputs. Then, the prediction was sent along with the true labels to the loss function. Base on the output of the loss function, the optimizer modified the model's parameters using a gradient-based method.

To prevent overfitting, drop-out layers were put after two pooling layers and the fully connected layer. The probability that each element is kept in those layers are respectively: 0.2, 0.3 and 0.5.

After finished all batches of a data file, the 'temporally' accuracy of the model is computed by sending all samples of the files into the model and calculating their predicted outputs. Notes that the purpose of this step is to just briefly check the model's accuracy, so the model only calculated the output of given samples. Loss function and optimizer were not fired, so there was no changes on current parameters of the model. Later, the accuracy was computed by comparing the predictions returned from the model to the true output from the labels files.

Theoretically, the training accuracies computed using data files will provide a plot like the blue line in Figure 3.7. Training and computing accuracy on the same dataset, the accuracy kept increasing until it reached 100

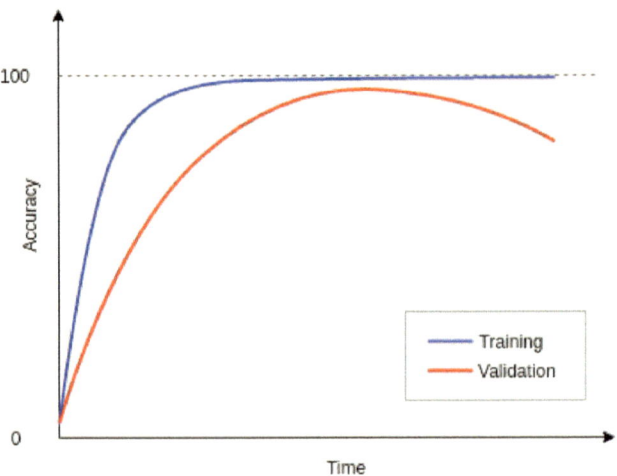

Figure 3.7: Training accuracy and validation accuracy

Then, the training process continued with the next files until all 15 files were learned. When one epoch was done, the network re-learned the training data again until it finished 20 epochs.

3.2.4   Validation and testing

3.2.4.1   Validation

At the end of each epoch, I validated the model by sending samples from the validation dataset (10 files) as input of the model. Just like computing the model's accuracy after each file, the model calculated samples output and return the result without learning the input. Then, comparing the predicted output from the model to the true validation labels, the program computed validation accuracy.

All validation accuracies and states of the model at the end of 20 epochs were saved. The curve of validation accuracy after each epoch is expected to looks similar to the red line in Figure 3.7. During the training process, the validation accuracy should keep increasing until a moment, it will stop raising or even start decreasing.

3.2.4.2   Testing

We know that the validation data files and training data files are isolated, so when the model is checked with validation dataset, we can assure that the validation accuracy expresses the performance of the network. In other words, the best state of the network is when it has the highest validation accuracy (the maximal of the red curve in Figure 3.7).

The model state which corresponds to the highest validation accuracy was chosen and loaded. Testing the model with input from the testing dataset, I received predicted output, then compared it with the true labels and computed the testing accuracy. This accuracy is considered as the final accuracy of the model. If this value is high, then the model will be concluded as a good one and vise versa.

3.3 Developing the network

In this section, I made some changes on the LeNet and observed how those changes affect the network. After that, I tried to combine some of those changes together to create a network which may perform better than the original one. The changes were applied on:

- Fully connected layer's width

- Convolutional kernels size

The results of those changes are shown and discussed in the next chapter.

Chapter 4

Results

In this chapter, the results of all the works that I have done in the previous chapter are given. Firstly, the results of the basic model were illustrated. After that, the results of the model under some modification and discussed on how the parameters of the model affected on it were shown. Finally, those results and drew out the best model for the problem were compared.

4.1 The basic network

4.1.1 Testing on the dataset

This section described the results of the first LeNet I have created in this project, to show that the network was well-constructed like what was explained in chapter 2 and it can be used for the classification problem of this project.

As being mentioned in Chapter 2, when a model is trained using a dataset, the training accuracy will increase until it reach 100%. However, validation data comes from another dataset so at the beginning, validation accuracy increased with training accuracy because it was underfitting, but when the overfitting occurred, the validation accuracy stop raising while training accuracy was continuously increasing. What happened for this network is suitable to the explanation of underfitting and overfitting in chapter 2 and the prediction in chapter 3.

Figure 4.1 displays the training accuracy and validation accuracy of my first network in the project.

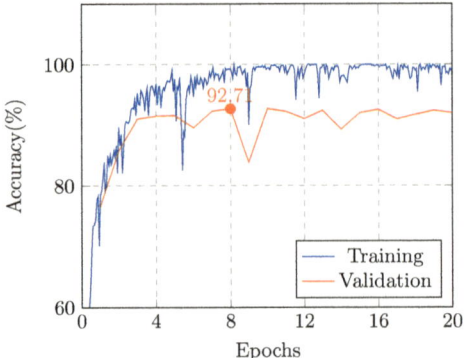

Figure 4.1: Training accuracy and Validation accuracy

There was a small difference between this result and the result in Figure 3.7, which is the validation accuracy in this figure did not strongly drop down as the red curve in the previous one. This can be explained by the similarity of the validation dataset and the training dataset. Normally, when a network becomes overfitting, its parameters start to be very "fit" to the training data so that its accuracy on other dataset becoming poor. However, in this case, it seems that the validation data shares a lot of similarities with the training data, so when the model is almost perfectly fit the training date, the validation accuracy is still high.

Among all validation accuracies, the highest one was 92.71%, found at step 120, which is epoch number 6th. I used the network state saved at this epoch to test with the testing data and the result of this state was considered as the testing accuracy of this model.

The testing result of the basic network is displayed in table VI:

Graph	Map	Photo	Hand-written text	Printed text	Average
92.72	91.21	90.02	94.27	93.48	92.68

Table VI: Testing accuracy of the network on classes (%)

From the table, it can be seen that the accuracies of the network when testing on five classes are not much different to each other. The network perform worse on dataset of the class Photo, but the accuracy is 90.02, which is acceptable.

4.1.2 Testing on real images

For testing, each image was divided into windows having size 224x224x3 to be the inputs of the network. Then, the network computed an output for each window. Each output was a vector of 5 values representing probabilities that the window belong to each class. After that, the average of all windows' outputs was computed and became the final output of the testing image.

The Figure 4.2 show images and the output of the classification computed by my first model and Table VII gives their output in numbers.

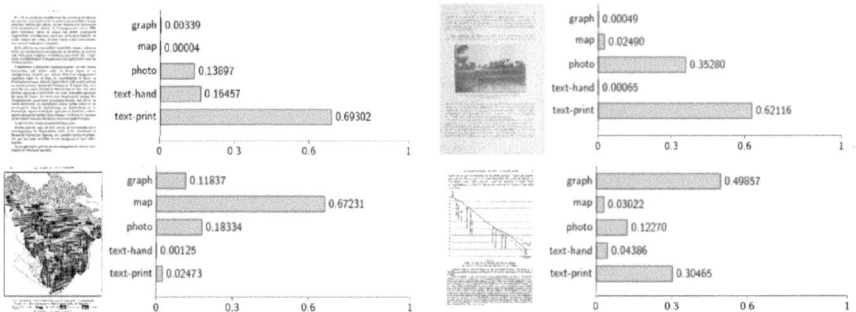

Figure 4.2: Test images and their output given by the network

As can be seen from the result, the probability of the predicted class always standouts of the others. For example, the first image which mostly covered by texts had the probability on class text-print much higher than the others. Images which is covered by more than one class had more than one pitches corresponding to those classes. The second testing image is an instance. About 50% of the image belongs to text-print class and 40% of photo, so the probabilities of those twos were 62% and 35%, which were much higher than the other. Interestingly, the probabilities is also corresponding to the percentage of area that the class covers on the testing images, but not very accurate. Hence, by looking at the testing result, we can say which class appears more on the image, not how many percents it covers.

Classes	Image 1	Image 2	Image 3	Image 4
Graph	0.00339	0.00049	0.11837	0.49857
Map	0.00004	0.02490	0.67231	0.03022
Photo	0.13897	0.35280	0.18334	0.12270
Text-hand	0.16457	0.00065	0.00125	0.04386
Text-print	069302	0.62116	0.02473	0.30465

Table VII: Test images and their output given by the network

4.2 The network modifications

By applying modifications on the original LeNet, some variants of the network has been created. This section displays the accuracies and compare them to the original one and to each other.

4.2.1 Fully connected layer

The network accuracies computed when changing the width of the fully connected layer are displayed in Figure 4.3. I intended to try width 128 for the this layer, but the program stop running because of the memory limitation. Thus, 64 is consider as the best width for the fully connected layer.

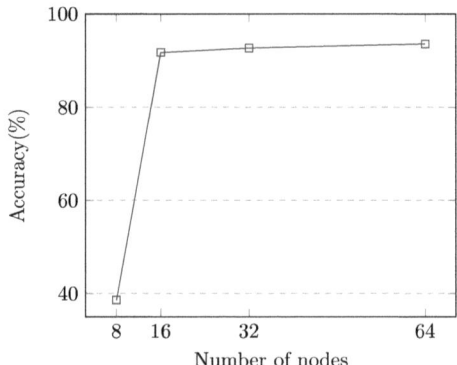

Figure 4.3: Network accuracy under the effect of fully connected layer's width

4.2.2 Convolutional layers

The network accuracy was changed when kernel sizes were modified. As can be seen from Figure 4.4, the network perform most well when the kernel size of the three convolutional layers are respectively 5x5, 7x7 and 3x3.

Assuming that the combination of those kernel size will result a better network, I tried creating a network which have the same structure as the original one, but three kernel sizes are 5x5, 7x7 and 3x3.

The accuracy of the new network was 93.06% not much different to the original, but took longer time to implement.

4.3 The new network

Combining all the best value of parameters from the previous modification, I created another network which also had three convolutional layers but with sizes respectively are 5x5, 7x7 and 3x3. The number

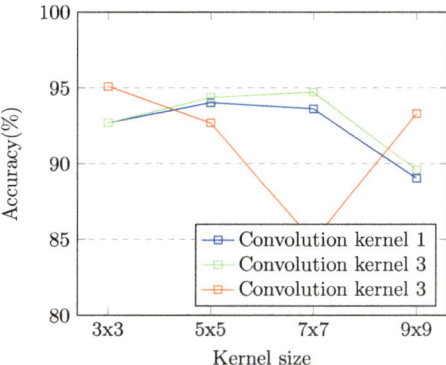

Figure 4.4: Network accuracy under the effect of convolution kernels

of neurons in the fully connected layer was increased to 64. This is a combination of values which were believed that increased the network performance, so I expected the new network would perform better than the original one.

Belows is the result of the new neural network and the comparison of it to the original LeNet.

Figure 4.5 compares the training accuracy of the new network to the original one. The figure shows that the training accuracy of the new network in 20 epochs was always lower than the first network. Both training accuracy and validation accuracy of the new network are lower than it previous version.

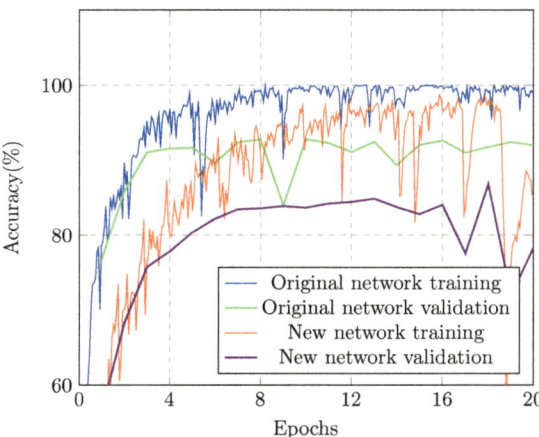

Figure 4.5: Training accuracy comparison between the original network and the new network

From this result, it can be concluded that, eventhough those changes which were separately made on the first model has increased its performance, it does not mean that the combination of them will result a better network.

Chapter 5

Conclusion

In this project, I created and augmented a dataset from a set of images to train a simple convolutional neural network which was expected to be able to classify documents to five given classes: graph, map, photo, hand-written text and printed text. The network contains three convolutional layers and a fully connected layer. After being trained, it was tested using testing dataset and got an accuracy 92.67% as the result. The network was also tested with real images and successfully classified them.

For developing the network, sizes of convolutional kernels in convolutional layers and the width of fully connected layer was modified. However, new networks did not perform much better than the original one and even worse when being combined together. Hence, the first convolutional neuron network of this project is still the best classifier for the problem.

Appendix A

Transfer functions

Name	Input/Output Relation	Icon	MATLAB Function
Hard Limit	$a = 0 \quad n < 0$ $a = 1 \quad n \geq 0$		hardlim
Symmetrical Hard Limit	$a = -1 \quad n < 0$ $a = +1 \quad n \geq 0$		hardlims
Linear	$a = n$		purelin
Saturating Linear	$a = 0 \quad n < 0$ $a = n \quad 0 \leq n \leq 1$ $a = 1 \quad n > 1$		satlin
Symmetric Saturating Linear	$a = -1 \quad n < -1$ $a = n \quad -1 \leq n \leq 1$ $a = 1 \quad n > 1$		satlins
Log-Sigmoid	$a = \dfrac{1}{1 + e^{-n}}$		logsig
Hyperbolic Tangent Sigmoid	$a = \dfrac{e^{n} - e^{-n}}{e^{n} + e^{-n}}$		tansig
Positive Linear	$a = 0 \quad n < 0$ $a = n \quad 0 \leq n$		poslin
Competitive	$a = 1 \quad$ neuron with max n $a = 0 \quad$ all other neurons	$\boxed{\mathbf{C}}$	compet

Table VIII: Transfer functions [5]

Bibliography

[1] ALONSO, J., AND CHEN, Y. Receptive field. *Scholarpedia 4*, 1 (2009), 5393. revision 136681.

[2] APHEX34. Typical CNN architecture, 2015. [Online; accessed September 2016].

[3] BAMPAROPOULOS, G. Statistical classification: A review on some techniques. University Lecture, 2012. [Online; accessed September 2016].

[4] GLOROT, X., BORDES, A., AND BENGIO, Y. Deep sparse rectifier neural networks. *Artificial Intelligence and Statistics (AISTATS)* (2011).

[5] HAGAN, M. T., AND DEMUTHS, H. B. *Neural Network Design 2nd Edition*. Martin Hagan, 2014.

[6] HEBB, D. *The Organization of Behavior*. New York: Wiley., 1949.

[7] HUBEL, D., AND WIESEL, T. Receptive fields and functional architecture of monkey striate cortex. *Journal of Physiology (London)* (1968), 215–243.

[8] ICTLAB. About ictlab. http://ictlab.usth.edu.vn/?page_id=366 [Accessed: Jul 2016].

[9] LECUN, O., BENGIO, Y., AND HINTON, G. Deep learning. *Nature* (2015), 436–444.

[10] LIBRARY, I. D. Convolution kernel, 2011. [Online; accessed September 2016].

[11] LOWEL, S., AND SINGER, W. *Machine Learning*. United States: American Association for the Advancement of Science, 1992.

[12] MCCULLOCH, W., AND PITTS, W. A logical calculus of ideas immanent in nervous activity. *Bulletin of Mathematical Biophysics.* (1943), 115–133.

[13] MITCHELL, T. *Machine Learning*. McGraw Hill, 1997.

[14] NAIR, V., AND HINTON, G. Rectified linear units improve restricted boltzmann machines. *International Conference on Machine Learning* (2010).

[15] ROSENBLATT, F. The perceptron: A probabilistic model for information storage and organization in the brain. *Psychological Review.* (1958), 386–408.

[16] RUSSELL, S. J., AND NORVIG, P. *Artificial Intelligence: A Modern Approach*. Upper Saddle River, New Jersey: Prentice Hall, 2009.

[17] SELFRIDGE, O. G. Pandemonium: a paradigm for learning in mechanisation of thought processes. *Proc. Symposium on Mechanisation of Thought Processes* (1958), 513–526.

[18] SRIVASTAVA, N., HINTON, G., KRIZHEVSKY, A., SUTSKEVER, I., AND SALAKHUTDINOV, R. Dropout: A simple way to prevent neural networks from overfitting. *Journal of Machine Learning Research 15* (2014), 1929–1958.

[19] VERLEYSEN, M., AND FRANÇOIS, D. *The Curse of Dimensionality in Data Mining and Time Series Prediction*. Springer Berlin Heidelberg, Berlin, Heidelberg, 2005, pp. 758–770.

[20] WERBOS, P. *Beyond Regression: New Tools for Prediction and Analysis in the Behavioral Sciences*. PhD thesis, Harvard University (1974).

YOUR KNOWLEDGE HAS VALUE